Symbols and Images in Church

By James E. Frazier

LOYOLAPRESS.

CHICAGO

LOYOLAPRESS.

3441 N. ASHLAND AVENUE
CHICAGO, ILLINOIS 60657
(800) 621-1008

Acknowledgments:
The Scripture quotations contained herein are from the New Revised
Standard Version Bible: Catholic Edition, copyright © 1993 and 1989
by the Division of Christian Education of the National Council of the
Churches of Christ in the U.S.A. Used by permission. All rights
reserved.

Cover image reprinted from *Clip Art for Year B* by Steve Erspamer.
Archdiocese of Chicago: Liturgy Training Publications, 1800 North
Hermitage Avenue, Chicago, Illinois 60622-1101. (800) 933-1800. All
rights reserved. Used with permission.

Interior Design: Megan Keane DeSantis
Cover Design: Shawn Biner

© 1997 Loyola Press

ISBN: 0-8294-0975-0

01 02 03 04 05 DataR 7 6 5 4 3

Contents

Introduction

C hristians have worshiped in various ways over the centuries. Language and culture influence worship. Shifts in beliefs and customs, and variations in Church leadership, also affect worship. If a nation's government is a friendly one, Christians can worship in public. But if the government is hostile, they must worship secretly or rebelliously.

The early Christians in Rome often met in underground catacombs for fear of persecution. They worshiped differently from Christians in the comfortable suburbs of America today. Christians in the cathedrals of medieval Europe worshiped differently from Christians on the American frontier. The Pilgrims in colonial New England worshiped differently from tribes in Christian Africa.

Some Christian groups worship in silence. Others worship noisily, and even boisterously, while some *sing* nearly everything. Some worship very simply while others follow complicated ceremonials. Some use statues and pictures of the saints; others forbid images of all types. Some Christians dance, clap their hands, and raise their arms in prayer and blessing; others are uncomfortable with gestures of any sort. Some wear ordinary street clothes while others wear vestments or the black gowns of college professors. Some churches observe strict orders of worship; others prefer to be free and creative. In wonderful and mysterious ways all of these go to make up the Body of Christ living and working in the world.

Out of this diversity, Roman Catholic worship emerges with a style of its own. In some ways it is similar to other types of Christian worship. In other ways it is quite different.

If we look closely at the symbols and images in a Catholic Church we get an idea of what makes worship Catholic. Of all these symbols, the ambo (from where Scripture is proclaimed), the baptistery, and the seating area for the congregation are the most important symbols that we see in nearly all Christian worship everywhere.

Let's get beyond these first impressions. Let's take a good look at the symbols and images we find, and discover what really makes our worship Catholic.

1 The Building

The building erected for public worship is a sign of the living Church. It is the largest of all our symbols. It is called a church, rather than an auditorium or a worship space, because it is a symbol of the Church that worships there. The building surrounds and shelters the place where a holy encounter occurs between God and the people of God. It is a public and civic sign for all the world to see.

A well-designed building plays a vital role in the liturgy. Its light and shadow, its acoustical properties, its spatial ordering to accommodate the hierarchical structure of the Church itself—all these contribute to the drama and beauty of the liturgy.

A few round churches have been constructed, like the medieval chapel of Charlemagne in Aachen, Germany, and the Temple Church in London. Some modern churches also have been built "in the round." Many churches take the form of the Greek or Latin cross. The basilican plan, which inspired centuries of church architecture, drew its inspiration from public buildings of the Roman Empire. A few examples survive in several of the oldest churches in Rome.

By an ancient tradition rooted in pagan nature religions, in Hebrew worship, and in the earliest baptismal rites, churches were historically orientated so that worshipers entered by a west door and worshiped facing east. Ezekiel describes worshipers in the Temple in this manner,

1

with "their faces toward the East, prostrating themselves to the sun toward the East" (Ezekiel 8:16).

Tourists to Europe and the Near East can see this orientation of churches everywhere. But by a remarkable exception, owing perhaps to its location west of Rome, Saint Peter's Basilica has a reverse orientation. One enters from the East and worships facing the West.

The English word *church* derives from the Greek *kyriakon*, meaning "belonging to the Lord." The word was applied originally to buildings set apart and belonging to the Lord for worship. But the Latin word for church, *ecclesia*, comes from another Greek word that means "assembly," primarily an assembly of self-governing citizens.

The symmetry and harmony of the parts of the ancient Hebrew tabernacle expressed divine perfection. Likewise, the church where Catholics worship symbolizes for them the splendor and beauty of the heavenly city. Architects and artists have significant roles to play in the design and construction of buildings "belonging to the Lord" and to the assembly.

2 The Congregation and the Nave

The largest symbols are among the most important, and the very ones we are likely to overlook. After the building itself, the largest symbol in any church, Catholic and non-Catholic alike, is the area for the congregation. This is where the baptized take their place to perform their solemn act of worship on the Lord's Day. Baptism entitles them and obligates them to this place.

We might overlook the importance of this area because we tend to equate the seating area in a church with the seating area in an ordinary auditorium or concert hall. But the difference could hardly be greater.

In a concert hall, those in the audience are spectators. They have heard about a performance, they pay a price for a more or less expensive seating area, they reserve a seat, they enjoy the performance on the stage, and they leave without obligation.

The congregation in a church, by contrast, responds to a divine call that makes no distinction between persons. Rich and poor, young and old, male and female, educated and uneducated alike take their place together. They pay no price, other than the price of conversion and discipleship. There are no reserved seats. They do not come as observers. They listen with commitment to the Scriptures, the homily, and the prayers. They inherit the Word, and they take it to heart. They receive the Body and Blood of Christ under the judgment of death but with the promise of resurrection. When they leave, they leave with the charge to make a difference in the world. A congregation is no ordinary audience.

From as early as the fourth century, and for centuries thereafter, congregations did not sit at public worship. Chairs and pews are a more recent development. In North America today, long immovable pews or benches are the norm. In Europe most congregations sit in movable chairs. If congregations had to stand all through Mass, worship would place heavy physical demands on us. But we would never mistake a congregation for an audience.

The area where the congregation assembles is often called the nave, a name that perhaps derives from the Latin word *navis*, for "ship." The church is symbolized in a ship. The nave of a traditional Romanesque or Gothic church resembles the hull of an old wooden ship, especially if its ceiling has heavy beams and timbers.

The nave is distinct from the elevated sanctuary where the vested ministers function at the ambo and the altar. For a long part of our history, the nave was separated from the sanctuary by an altar rail or, in medieval cathedrals, by an ornamental stone or carved wooden screen. In more contemporary churches, especially those "in the round," there is less distinction between the nave and the sanctuary. But the sanctuary is always distinguished from the nave in some way, either by being elevated or by its design and furnishings.

On an average Sunday morning in most churches, the congregation consists not only of active parish members whose life in Christ is a vital reality for them but of a wide range of other people as well. Some are just curious. Some are seekers. Others are catechumens preparing for baptism, doubters wanting to believe, former believers struggling to believe again, or fallen-away believers who want to give good example to their children. They all belong to the Body of Christ, and all have a place in the congregation. They are a symbol of Christ in the world.

All Christians are baptized into the same Christ, and all are prophets, priests, and kings by baptism. The Church is therefore a unity, and there are no distinctions of persons.

Nevertheless, the building up of the Church depends on its ordering into a hierarchy. We can see this hierarchical ordering best when the Church assembles for the Eucharist. There the assignment of particular people or groups of people to perform particular duties is most evident. Everyone in the Church is responsible for exercising his or her particular gifts and for performing the duties proper to his or her place in the Church's ordering. The laity have duties to fulfill at Eucharist distinct from the duties of those ordered as deacons, priests, and bishops.

Some members of the congregation exercise their gifts as readers, eucharistic ministers, cantors, choir members, ushers, or acolytes. Those lacking gifts for liturgical ministry nevertheless have other gifts that help to build up the Church. They are teachers, auto mechanics, bus drivers, parents, artists, scientists, and journalists. To the extent that they are putting their gifts to use in the world, they are exercising their ministry as laity in the Church.

Catholicism has held firmly to the belief that in the Mass Christ becomes really present in the consecrated bread and wine. But in 1963 Vatican II reminded us that there are many modes in which Christ is present in the Church. Christ is present in works of mercy and whenever the Church prays and sings. He promised to be present "where two or three are gathered in my name" (Matthew 18:20).

Christ is therefore present in the assembled congregation, and the place where they assemble is a holy place. An *empty* nave is a sign of the holiness of the world in which the scattered congregation lives and works the other six days of the week. Christ is present among them while they fulfill their Christian duties dispersed throughout their communities. It is not they who live, but Christ who lives in them (Galatians 2:20). And whatever good they do, even to the very least, they do to Christ (Matthew 25:40).

Whether assembled in the church or dispersed in the world, the congregation is an image of the living Christ.

3 The Presider and the Chair

Whenever the congregation gathers to worship, someone always presides in the person of Christ. The presider prays in the name of the entire holy people and of all present in the assembly. The one presider symbolizes the unity of the Church under the headship of Christ. The presider at Mass offers the same sacrifice offered by Christ the high priest, who offered himself once on the cross.

When Vatican II declared Christ to be present in the assembly and in the eucharistic bread and wine, it also affirmed Christ's presence in the person of the minister who presides in his name.

The presider at Mass must be an ordained bishop or priest. For other services, like morning prayer, evening prayer, baptisms, weddings, funeral rites (except for Mass), and holy communion in the absence of a priest, the presider can be a deacon. In some instances the presider can be a designated lay person.

The chair from which the bishop or priest presides is a symbol of his teaching office, of his oversight of the Church, and of his presiding over the assembly at worship.

In the earliest centuries of the Church, the chair stood in the center of the apse facing the assembly. In later centuries it was moved to the side of the sanctuary. The reforms in our day have returned the chair to its ancient position facing the congregation.

The name of the bishop's church, the cathedral, comes from the Latin word *cathedra*, meaning "chair." But the chair of even the smallest parish church symbolizes the same apostolic faith that bishops and priests are obligated to preserve and teach the world over.

When the pope makes pronouncements on matters of faith and morals with the fullest authority of his office, he is said to be speaking *ex cathedra*, or "from the chair."

The Church observes the Feast of the Chair of Saint Peter on February 22. The chair figures in this feast because it symbolizes the fact that Peter was the first bishop to preside over the Church of Rome. The Church prays that its faith may always be as strong as the rock on which Peter confessed and died for his faith.

Saint Peter's Basilica in the Vatican City is the largest church in Christendom. But it is not a cathedral in the technical sense. It is the church of the pope as pastor of the universal Catholic Church.

As bishop of Rome, the pope presides from the chair in the Basilica of Saint John Lateran, the cathedral for the Diocese of Rome proper. The Lateran was the official residence of the popes from the fourth century until their departure to France in the fourteenth century.

4 The Altar and the Ambo

THE ALTAR

The altar is the primary symbol for the Eucharist, the central act of Christian worship. Of all the objects in a Catholic Church, the altar is the one that has most symbolized Catholic worship through the centuries. It is a sign of Christ himself, who is the victim, the priest, and the altar of his own sacrifice. Catholics show the altar great reverence.

As members of the Body of Christ, Christians are also spiritual altars on which the sacrifice of a holy life is offered to God. They are the living stones out of which the Lord Jesus builds the Church.

At the altar the congregation presents the sacrifice of its life and labor. And there they receive the gifts of God won for them by Christ. In the giving and the receiving, God is glorified, and the Church is sanctified.

Very few objects are absolutely essential for the Lord's Supper. On a battlefield or under repression, Catholic worship has often had to forego vestments, chair, ambo, candles, crucifix, and incense. But a simple table of even modest proportion is a practical necessity.

In the earliest years of Christian worship, altars were freestanding, like ordinary tables, and were made of wood. But during the Roman persecutions, Christians sometimes erected altars over the graves of martyrs, and they celebrated the Eucharist there. These fixed, permanent altars were made of stone. Over time, altars came to be elaborately carved and decorated. In subsequent centuries, altars were placed against the distant wall of the sanctuary and were surrounded by statues and stone or wooden carvings.

After the persecutions, the bodies of saints, even non-martyrs, continued in some places to be placed under altars as a matter of course. Until 1977 the relics of a martyr, or other saint, were required to be placed beneath all altars in Roman Catholic churches, or to be encased in a stone set within the altar. New altars erected today are not required to contain relics, but the practice of entombing them below an altar (not in the table top) is encouraged.

With the recent liturgical reforms, altars are again preferably freestanding, to permit walking around them and to permit the priest to face the people. The altar is placed in such a way as to be the focal point of the whole congregation. Ordinarily the altar used for Mass is fixed, not portable, and it is consecrated. New altars today are often again made of wood.

Before Vatican II it was common to erect at least three altars in a church, and sometimes many more, depending on the size of the church and the number of priests assigned to the parish. The lesser "side" altars were used for so-called private Masses without a congregation, and the "high" altar was used for Masses with a congregation.

A single altar in a church is preferable to numerous altars. The single altar signifies the one savior, Jesus Christ, and the one Eucharist of the Church in the one assembly of God's holy people.

When Catholics enter or leave a church, they show reverence to the altar by making a profound bow to it. They also bow to it whenever they pass in front of it. The clergy, acolytes, and other liturgical ministers bow to the altar when they approach it. The priest and deacon also kiss the altar at the beginning and ending of Mass.

As the central act of Christian worship, the Mass focuses on the pivotal event in the life of Jesus: the three-day period that included his last supper, his crucifixion and death, and his rising to life. It is at the altar that the Church celebrates this paschal mystery, as it is called. And it is there that the Church finds the source and the summit of all its work and worship.

On the night before Jesus died, he sat at table for supper with the apostles. He told them to share the bread and cup in his memory (Luke 22:19; 1 Corinthians 11:24–25). He identified the wine as his blood and the bread as his body (Matthew 26:26–28; Mark 14:22–24; Luke 22:19–20; 1 Corinthians 11:24–25). When Jesus asked his disciples if they could drink the cup he was about to drink (Matthew 20:22), he was really asking if they were willing to suffer with him.

Catholics share this same meal at the Church's altar, but they also offer the sacrifice Christ offered the next day on the cross. The Mass is both a banquet and a sacrifice. The Lord's Supper, therefore, is no ordinary meal, and the altar is no ordinary table.

The Church calls this sacrificial meal the Lord's Supper, the Mass, or Holy Communion. The word Eucharist is also common today. It comes from the Greek word for thanksgiving. The Mass is the supreme act of thanksgiving to God for the creation and the redemption of the world through Christ.

Among the Hebrews, sacrifice was made in the Temple at Jerusalem until its destruction in A.D. 70, and the chief sacrifice was that of the paschal lamb sacrificed for each household at Passover. Scripture identifies Christ as the new Paschal Lamb, the new victim, slain on the cross for the redemption of the whole world.

The difference between altars and tables is not just one of material. An altar is a table used specifically for offering sacrifice. In world religions that have practiced sacrifice, the altar is where the victim is offered. A Christian altar, then, is the table set apart for the offering of Christ's sacrifice.

Catholics hold that the Eucharist is the same sacrifice as that of Christ on Calvary. For them, it is not a *repeating* of the sacrifice. It is the *same* sacrifice. Catholic tradition has, therefore, preferred the word *altar*, although the word *table*, or *altar table*, is now used by some Catholics as well.

Catholic tradition observes the supper of the Lord every Sunday, if not even daily. It does so in Christ's memory, but it also believes that the Lord's Supper is not just a past event. It is a present event as well. The Orthodox Church and the Episcopal Church hold this belief along with Roman Catholics.

Like many other Christians, Catholics believe that their faith is nourished by remembering the words of Jesus at his last supper and by repeating his actions as he commanded. But they believe further that in consuming the eucharistic bread and wine, they actually receive his Body and Blood. With the apostle Paul, Catholics believe that the cup of blessing that we bless is a communion with the blood of Christ, and the bread that we break is a communion with the body of Christ (1 Corinthians 10:16–17).

Many non-Catholics interpret Jesus' instructions differently. Some observe the Lord's Supper only rarely, perhaps as few as four times a year. Many of them believe that communion is simply a remembering of the words and actions of Jesus. They believe that by repeating the words and actions of Jesus, their own faith is nourished. But they generally do not believe they have a real sharing in the actual Body and Blood of Christ.

Catholic laity for many centuries received Communion only once a year—not unlike some Protestants even today. They attended Mass regularly, said their private devotions, adored the Eucharist, and made what was called a *spiritual* communion. But they rarely received Holy Communion. The priest alone received Communion at every Mass.

For many centuries Catholics received Communion only under the form of bread. They were not given the sacramental wine to drink. The priest alone received both the bread and the cup. In the sixteenth century, the Council of Trent taught that in receiving Communion in the form of bread alone Catholics receive Christ, whole and entire, with all the effects of God's grace. It did not seem to be necessary to receive the chalice.

Vatican II restored communion from the cup to the Catholic laity. Holy Communion has a more complete form as a sacramental sign when it is received under both kinds. Protestants have always received both the bread and the cup for communion.

The bread used for the Catholic Eucharist is made of wheat flour and water alone. In keeping with the Jewish use of unleavened bread at Passover, and the age-old custom of the Latin Church, no leavening is added to the eucharistic bread. The wine must be from the fruit of the vine. It is natural and pure and contains no other substance.

It was ancient practice for Christians to receive communion in the hand. The practice has been restored after some centuries of reception on the tongue. But each communicant has the option to receive Communion either in the hand or on the tongue. The two ways of receiving the sacrament can take place during the same liturgical service without causing discord in the family of God.

THE AMBO

The ambo is the place where the Word of God is proclaimed by the readers, sung by the cantor, and interpreted by the deacon or priest. The ambo also can be used for reciting or singing the general intercessions, the Church's prayer for the needs of the whole world.

Like the altar, the ambo is a place where God engages in a solemn encounter with the Church. With the altar, it is a primary symbol in the central act of Christian worship and a focal point for the assembly's attention.

The ambo figures prominently at the Easter Vigil. From the ambo the readers proclaim eight accounts from the history of salvation, the cantor sings eight psalms, and the deacon or priest proclaims the Gospel of the Resurrection. The Exsultet, also called the Easter proclamation, can be proclaimed from the ambo as well.

An ambo is an enclosed platform, with a standing reading desk (sometimes called a lectern), made usually of wood or stone. It is elevated to facilitate ease of hearing and seeing by the congregation. Sometimes it is called the pulpit. The word ambo was originally used for pulpits erected in early Roman churches.

In the earliest times the bishop preached from his chair. Only later did he use the ambo. Today the presider may preach either from the ambo or from the chair, but the ambo is the ordinary place.

After God spoke to Jacob in a dream and declared, "I am the Lord," Jacob awoke and said, "Surely the Lord is in this place." He marked the place of his encounter with a stone (Genesis 28:10–22). Jesus himself frequently taught or preached in synagogues, both in his hometown and elsewhere (Matthew 13:54; Mark 6:1–2; Luke 4:16; John 6:59).

The ambo in a church is like Jacob's stone and the pulpit in a synagogue. The congregation goes to it often, expecting to encounter the living God again and again.

The first part of the Mass is called the liturgy of the word. It takes place at the ambo and has similarities to the synagogue service. Both services consist of readings from Scripture, prayer, singing, and a homily. Both services require an ambo but not an altar. Adult catechumens being prepared for baptism in the Catholic Church traditionally attend this first part of the Mass but leave before the liturgy of the Eucharist begins at the altar. The first part of the Mass also resembles the service in Protestant churches when Communion is not celebrated.

On Sundays and other solemnities Catholics hear three passages from Scripture. The first is usually from the Old Testament. The second is from the New Testament epistles, the Acts of the Apostles, or the Book of Revelation. The third is from one of the Gospels. Between the readings, the cantor sings verses from the psalms, with the congregation singing a recurring antiphon.

The readings, the sung psalms, and the homily ordinarily take place at the ambo. Sometimes for convenience the various functions of reading, singing, and preaching take place at several different locations. In fact, many older churches have a smaller ambo for the readings and a larger ambo for preaching. The cantor sometimes sings from a third place still.

When we take it to heart, the Word proclaimed from the ambo can turn life around for us. The ambo is where the story of salvation history is recounted, revealing the plan of God for the world and those who live in it. Like the altar, the presider, and the congregation, the ambo is a place where the presence of God becomes manifest in the church.

For many centuries of Catholic worship, there were only two readings at Mass, not three. The priest usually read them quietly in Latin, at the altar rather than the ambo, with his back to the congregation. The readings were not audible to the people in the nave. Preaching was rare. Before the advent of inexpensive commercial printing, which enabled the congregation to read English translations of the Latin from their missals, the congregation at Sunday Mass encountered the scriptural Word of God only with difficulty.

Vatican II restored the primitive practice of the Church. Three readings, sung psalms, participation by lay readers and a deacon, and a homily—all in English—are now normative for Sunday Mass. Catholics now have the same privilege of hearing the Word of God proclaimed and interpreted in their own language, and with the same direct power, that has been the privilege of the Protestant traditions for over 400 years.

5 The Lectionary and the Sacramentary

The Word of God is not just the expression of God's thoughts and ideas. It is not just holy speech or rules about how to live. Nor is it just a collection of religious stories or reports about miracles.

Instead, the Word is the living and personal action of God in the world. It causes things to happen. It creates order out of chaos and chaos out of order. It turns deserts into gardens and gardens into deserts. It penetrates hardened hearts and gives comfort where there is worry and stress. It turns the world around and tears down rigid structures that have become self-serving.

We do not sit back and listen passively to the Word. Those who truly hear the Word of God listen to it passionately. They cannot help but be changed.

Christians and Jews alike believe that the Word has gathered them into a nation of holy people. The Word binds them together as a family and promises them faithfulness through thick and thin.

The Word that made a beautiful world out of chaos, and led the nation of Israel from slavery to freedom, is the same Word that made a young Jewish virgin into the Mother of God. The Word became flesh in Jesus, the child of that virgin. When we hear the Word of God, we take our place alongside all who have ever been turned around by it. Some of our predecessors in the faith went to their death because the Word of God was that important to them.

Christians believe that they have access to the Word of God in the collection of books called the Bible. There they find the accounts of God's dealings with the world and its inhabitants. They encounter the gentle love of a God who pursues those who have turned their backs and rebelled. They hear the prophets scolding the complacent in the name of God. They hear the praises and laments of the psalmist, and they encounter God's wisdom in the wisdom writings. But the Word of God is not primarily a book to be read.

Like their Jewish brothers and sisters, Christians have a high regard for the written word because it preserves the acts of the living Word for telling from generation to generation. Jewish tradition preserves its Scriptures in ceremonial scrolls that represent the Word of God in the Law, or the Torah. The scrolls contain the first five books of the Hebrew Scriptures.

The Christian Bible collects into one volume all the Hebrew Scriptures (the Law, the Prophets, and the Writings), also called the Old Testament, together with the New Testament, its four Gospels, the Acts of the Apostles, the letters, and the Book of Revelation. The Bible is the Word of God for Christians of all denominations (although not all agree on which books comprise the Bible).

Because the Bible is a book, we might think of the liturgy of the word, at the beginning of Mass, as a reading session or a Bible class, with everyone taking time to do their private Bible study. This is not the case.

The Word of God is not primarily a book to be read. The Bible is God's proclamation to the world. The readings at Mass are, therefore, manifestations of God in the hearing of the Church. They are incarnations of the Word among us. They come to us through proclamations like those of the Hebrew prophets, who spoke on behalf of God, giving words of comfort and condemnation. In short, the readings are actions.

It sometimes surprises Christians unfamiliar with Catholic worship to learn that Catholics do not use the Bible at Mass. This fact has sometimes led to misunderstandings about the place of the Bible in the Catholic Church. As long as the readings at Mass were said inaudibly and in Latin, it was easy for non-Catholics to think that Mass excluded the scriptural Word of God. But today anyone attending Mass can see how Bible-centered Catholic worship really is.

The book that Catholics use at Mass instead of the Bible is called the *lectionary*. The lectionary simply takes the biblical readings assigned for the Church year and prints them in a convenient order for easier use by the various readers.

In the Middle Ages, before the invention of the printing press, all books had to be hand-lettered with pen and ink on parchment or animal skin. Many of these beautiful books were elaborately ornamented with colorful pigments and illuminated with gold leaf. They were bound in impressive bindings. Monks in monasteries were masters of the book arts.

The medieval gospel books, or evangelaries, are stunning examples of the bookmaker's art and craft. Among the finest of these precious works are the *Book of Kells* and the *Lindisfarne Gospels*, the work of eighth-century Irish monks. Through their beauty our eyes enjoy a glimpse of the same glory that our ears hear in the Word proclaimed from the ambo.

Like the scrolls of the Torah in the synagogue service, the lectionary is treated with respect befitting the Word of God. It is held aloft in procession and, like the altar, it is kissed by the deacon or priest who reads from it.

Vatican II revised the order of readings at Mass and devised a three-year cycle so that over time the laity would hear a larger portion of the Bible. The purpose was to arouse in the Church a greater hunger for the Word of

God, so that all would be better nourished at the table of God's Word.

The lectionary includes a first reading, the psalm or canticle, a second reading, the verse for the Gospel acclamation, and the Gospel. Three readings and parts of two psalms are read on every Sunday and solemnity of the Church year.

The lectionary is not the only book used at Mass. The *sacramentary* is the book used by the bishop, the priest, and the deacon. It contains all the prayers said or sung by the presider. It does not contain the readings. An acolyte often holds the sacramentary for the presider at the chair so he can read from it more easily. During the liturgy of the Eucharist the sacramentary is placed on the altar so the presider can read from it.

The sacramentary in use today is the one authorized in 1970 by Pope Paul VI following the decrees of Vatican II. The official edition is in Latin, which is still the first language for Roman Catholic worship. The Mass today, all of it or just part of it, can technically be said or sung in Latin. But the sacramentary has been translated into virtually all the world's languages so that Roman Catholics everywhere can worship in their own tongue.

Prior to 1970, the sacramentary in use for 400 years was the Roman Missal authorized in 1570 by Saint Pius V following a decree of the Council of Trent. This is the source of the so-called Tridentine Mass. The Missal of Trent was in Latin, and it was never permitted to be used in any other language. For hundreds of years Catholics worshiped in a language they did not easily understand.

The Church had used many other sacramentaries over the centuries prior to the Council of Trent. The oldest surviving sacramentary is found in a seventh-century manuscript. It is called the Leonine Sacramentary in honor of Pope Saint Leo the Great, who died in 461.

The readers and the presiders are not the only ones to use books in Catholic worship. The congregation also uses a book containing what they need to say and sing for the Eucharist.

The official "hymnal" for Mass is called the *Roman Gradual*. It contains all of the music properly sung by the congregation at the Eucharist for every day of the Church year. It is impractical for most parishes, however, because it is completely in Latin and contains only Gregorian chant, with its four-line staves and square notes. Its use is practically restricted to those monasteries that choose to celebrate the Mass in Latin.

Most U.S. parishes today use some type of hardcover or paperbound service book in English. It may be a hymnal or service book, or a music supplement. Some of these books contain music composed for the Church over the last 300 years, but most of it was composed in the past 20 years.

Unlike all other major Christian bodies in North America, Catholics do not have an official hymnal in English. Each parish is free to choose from a number of books available from several publishers. As a result, the music that Catholics sing at Mass can be quite different from parish to parish.

Some Catholics bring a small missal of their own from home. These missals were once very popular among Catholics. As a rule, they do not contain music. Their purpose is identical to that of the *Book of Common Prayer* that Episcopalians use. The people's missal contains all the texts of the Mass, so that the congregation can take their full and active part in public worship.

Catholic worship makes use of all these books not because the Mass is a literary event but because our memory is not keen enough to remember all the changing liturgical texts. The books are prompters for our roles at Eucharist. They enable us to conduct our worship with dignity and in good order. They also help to ensure a certain unity in Catholic worship, from parish to parish, and from region to region.

6 The Baptistery

The baptistery is the place where people are baptized. It is a symbol of washing, of death, and of rebirth. In the waters of the baptistery, the new Christian enters the Church by faith, in the name of the Father, the Son, and the Holy Spirit. Baptism represents the believer's first sacramental encounter with the transforming power of God in the Church. The virtually universal practice of baptism among Christians makes the baptistery a symbol of Christian unity across denominational lines.

In most churches the baptistery is simply a font. It is made of stone or metal and is found at the main entrance to the church. Sometimes it is placed in or near the sanctuary, where it can be seen by the congregation. In newer churches the baptistery is sometimes constructed as a shallow pool in the floor, so that those being baptized have to step down into it. It can be located in a gathering space, like a large vestibule, or just inside the doors of the nave itself.

Immersion is the preferred form of baptism because of its fuller symbol of washing. But infusion, or pouring, is also permissible.

From as early as the third century, the baptistery was a distinct building separate from the church itself. It stood adjacent to the church, or just outside the church's main west doors, as a sign that one enters the Church through the baptistery.

Baptisteries were often octagonal to reflect the eighth day of the week on which Jesus rose from the dead and the fullness of time in the kingdom of God. As the intermediate form between the square and the circle, the octagon is a symbol of regeneration. In the Middle Ages the number eight was a symbol of the waters of baptism.

Many baptisteries have richly ornamented interiors, with brilliant mosaics depicting the baptism of Christ in the Jordan River and biblical scenes related to spiritual birth and nurture. Entering such a baptistery is like entering a garden paradise with the sound of running water.

One of the oldest baptisteries is that at Saint John Lateran Basilica in Rome, the cathedral of the Diocese of Rome. Its baptistery dates from the time of the fourth-century emperor Constantine.

A more famous baptistery is the one in Florence, Italy, standing outside the entrance to the cathedral. With origins in the fifth or sixth century, the baptistery was much altered in subsequent times. Michelangelo is said to have called its magnificent bronze doors the "Gates of Paradise."

Whether baptism takes place in a splendid building, at a simple font, or in a river, it is indeed the passage into a garden where living water flows.

Like other Jews of his day, John the Baptist proclaimed a baptism of repentance for the forgiveness of sin (Mark 1:4). When he baptized Jesus in the river Jordan, the voice of the Father declared Jesus to be his Son, and the Holy Spirit descended on him in the form of a dove (Mark 1:9–11). His baptism by John had trinitarian significance, but Jesus had no sin and no need for forgiveness. His baptism signified his solidarity with repentant humanity.

In a conversation with Nicodemus, Jesus announced that one could not enter the kingdom of God except by water *and the Spirit* (John 3:5). Jesus himself baptized (John 3:22), and he told his disciples to do likewise, in the name of the Father, the Son, and the Holy Spirit

(Matthew 28:19). Jesus' act of baptism was clearly different from that of John.

Jesus used the word *cup* (Matthew 26:39) and the word *baptism* to refer to his turmoil and suffering (Mark 10:38; Luke 12:50). For the new believer, baptism often follows a crisis, a conversion, or a period of soul-searching. Indeed the apostle Paul taught that in baptism the believer experiences the death of Jesus and dies to himself and therefore experiences new life in the resurrection of Jesus (Romans 6:3–11). Baptism is not undertaken casually or lightly but requires the decision of a lifetime. Baptism is a rebirth, a starting over.

According to Saint Paul, baptism actually *causes* the believer's union with Christ and is a sure sign of it (Romans 6:4). Through it the believer is incorporated into the Body of Christ (1 Corinthians 12:13).

Even though there is no sure scriptural authority for the baptism of infants (although some interpret Acts 10:44–48 to include children), Jesus did tell his disciples to let the children come to him (Mark 10:14; Luke 18:16). And it is true that Scripture calls the children of Christian parents "holy" (1 Corinthians 7:14) and that nowhere does Scripture suggest that these children will later have to seek baptism as mature adults.

After the biblical era there is clear evidence of the baptism of children and infants. From at least the third century until the sixteenth-century Reformation, children born to Christian parents were baptized as infants. Lutherans, Episcopalians, Presbyterians, and Congregationalists still practice infant baptism. Sometimes the baptism is thought of more as a dedication of the child, with full membership in the Church reserved till a later and individual profession of mature faith. Baptists and some other Protestants do not practice infant baptism.

By ancient practice, baptism in the Catholic Church is associated with the Easter Vigil to bring out its paschal character. To the extent practical, adult baptism is reserved for this most solemn liturgy of the Church year, although in large parishes it is sometimes impractical to delay all baptisms until the Easter Vigil.

Infants are still frequently baptized during "private" services on Sunday afternoons attended only by the immediate family. This, however, diminishes the community aspect of baptism. Baptism not only washes the believer of sin but incorporates the believer into the Body of Christ. It is good, therefore, for the whole congregation to witness baptism at a community Eucharist since they also have obligations to fulfill in regard to the newly baptized.

An adult wanting baptism first becomes what is called a catechumen and passes through various stages of entry into the Church. The process of becoming formed in the mind of Christ is slow, and it follows rituals that have ancient roots in the practices of the Church. This so-called *catechumenate* had been abandoned for centuries but was restored in 1962. Today the catechumenate is mandatory for adult baptism.

7 The Paschal Candle

The paschal candle is the large candle that plays a central role in the liturgy of the Easter Vigil. It is placed on a candlestick that stands on the floor of the sanctuary throughout the Easter season. After Pentecost the candle is moved to the baptistery where it is lit for baptisms. It is placed next to the coffin at funerals. The paschal candle is also called the Easter candle, or the Christ candle.

The word *paschal* comes from Aramaic and Greek words referring to the Jewish Passover. Christians use the word paschal for the Feast of Easter, which is the Christian Passover. They also use the words *paschal mystery* to refer to the Passover of Jesus from death to life. Through baptism into the paschal mystery of Christ, Christians pass over from death to life again.

When the Israelites were freed from Egypt, the Lord led them with a pillar of cloud by day and a pillar of fire by night (Exodus 13:21; 14:24). The pillar represented the saving presence of God during the Passover of the Israelites from slavery in Egypt to freedom in the promised land.

The paschal candle represents Christ, the pillar of fire who brings all nations out of darkness into light and leads the newly baptized from darkness into light.

In an optional ritual at the beginning of the Easter Vigil, the presider inscribes the paschal candle with the sign of the cross. He marks it with the first and last letters of the Greek alphabet, the alpha and the omega, representing Christ, who is the first and the last. He inscribes the candle with the four digits of the year and inserts five grains of incense into the cross, representing the wounds of Christ. He then lights the candle from the new fire struck at the beginning of the liturgy.

The candle is carried in procession, and at three stations the processional stops for the deacon or cantor to chant "Christ our light." Standing in its light, the deacon or cantor then sings the Easter proclamation called the Exsultet, a long, beautiful text with roots as far back as the seventh century. The chant to which it is sung is one of the Church's finest. Its melodies are used only for this liturgy on this most holy night of the year.

In an optional gesture later in the service, the presider plunges the base of the candle three times into the water, breaking the water of the Church's womb and opening salvation to those wanting baptism.

The Church uses many candles in addition to the paschal candle. Before the days of electricity, all the light for the Church's worship was provided by burning wax on candlesticks or oil in lamps. A candle or a lamp was the only way to dispel the darkness. It was a practical necessity.

Candles are required at all public worship in a Catholic church, as a sign of reverence and festiveness. Two, four, or six candles are placed on or near the altar for Mass. A seventh is to be used when the bishop of the diocese presides. Candles are carried in processions, especially in Gospel processions.

Tapers are given to the newly baptized and to those attending the Easter Vigil and the Candlemas procession on the Feast of the Presentation (February 2). All the candles we use at worship are reflections of the Christ candle at the Easter Vigil.

The candles carried in procession to light the way of the church, the candles at the altar for Mass, and those used at the Gospel procession all signify for us the presence of Christ who is the light of the world.

In some churches four or twelve candles are placed in sconces around the church at the places where the church was anointed on the day of its dedication.

The candles used for morning prayer, evening prayer, and compline are especially significant because in those offices we name Christ as the morning star, the light that overcomes darkness, "the light of revelation to the Gentiles, and the glory of your people Israel."

When the sacrament is carried in procession, as on Holy Thursday, candles both light the way and signify the approaching presence of Christ. The sanctuary lamp, the candle that burns continuously in front of the tabernacle, often in a red glass container, is a living symbol of the abiding presence of Christ in the Blessed Sacrament.

In many Catholic, Orthodox, and Episcopal churches, a bank of small candles in glass containers called vigil lights, or tapers standing in sand, are placed in front of a statue, in a place set apart for meditation. A person may kneel there in prayer and light a candle, whose burning keeps the prayer, the pleading, and the intercession alive for as long as the flame has life, sometimes for days. Contributions of money may be made there to help with the cost of the candles, not to "buy" God's good favor.

8 Water, Oil, Fire, and Incense

C atholics delight in using earthy materials at worship. They anoint people and objects with oil, they pour and sprinkle water, they drink wine, they eat bread, they burn incense, they light fires, they wear beautiful garments, they collect money in baskets, and they carry books from place to place.

As a result, Catholic worship is not always tidy and neat. The water is wet; the oil is slippery; the fire leaves ashes; and the smoke makes breathing difficult and gets in your eyes. Hands get messy, things spill, and cups and plates need cleaning. But these inconveniences are minor compared to the awesome mysteries they help us to celebrate.

Catholic worship is earthy because God has been manifest and known through material creation from the very beginning of the history of salvation. God, in fact, *acts* through material creation. When God said, "Let there be light," there *was* light.

Just as the Israelites escaping Egypt recognized God in the parting of the Red Sea, and knew the manna as bread from heaven, so on the road to Emmaus the disciples recognized the risen Jesus when they saw him breaking bread.

When Christians eat bread and drink wine at the altar, and hear the Word proclaimed from the ambo, they don't see ordinary bread and wine or hear ordinary words. By their faith, Catholics see and taste God in the bread and wine. In the words they hear the Word of God. In the same way that the Israelites saw more than a break in the

water and the disciples more than the broken bread,
Catholics see, hear, touch, taste, and smell God through
the use they make of material things.

This is why Catholics hold the material world in such
reverence. They bow before the stone of the altar, and
they drink wine reverently. In pouring water over a new
believer, they see death and birth. When they burn
incense they see and smell the glory and sweetness of
God. Catholics revere the world because in it God is both
hidden and revealed.

When Catholics take these elements from the Earth,
and embrace them with words of praise, supplication, and
lament, and with reverent gestures, we call such worship
sacramental. What we mean is that the visible, material
creation is for us a sign of the invisible action of God in
our lives. For us it is difficult to separate the visible
material elements from the invisible presence and action
of God.

But although Catholics believe that God acts through
material elements when they use them sacramentally, they
do not practice a magical control over God. God is always
free to act independently of the Church's objects, words,
and gestures. God's goodness and love, and the gift of salvation, cannot be merited or earned through any human
action, not even by a sacramental action of the Church.
No one, not even the Church, deserves the grace of God
or wins it, except through the merits of Christ.

The sacramental character of Catholic worship is similar in some ways to the work of poets, artists, musicians,
and architects. These creative and visionary people select
stuff from creation. They take stone, clay, and metal, tone
and pitch, color and light, wood, words, paper, and fabric.
Indeed, they take virtually anything they can see or hear in
creation. Then they mold it and reshape it. They chip
away at it, they heat it, they bend it, and they rephrase it.

They take away from it, and they reorganize it. They juxtapose volumes and voids. In a word, they transform creation. Through their treatment and handling of their material, they make splendid forms out of the Earth's elements. In the splendor of these forms we see and hear glimpses of things unseen and unheard.

So at worship, Catholics take bread, they break it and share it, they pour wine and they drink it together, in such a way that these elements of Earth become splendid forms of things unseen, manifestations of things hidden, and disclosures of the unimaginable. The sense of mystery and awe that characterizes Catholic worship comes from this reverent use of elements from the material world and from the ancient words and gestures that embrace them.

WATER

Water has many uses in our daily lives. We drink it, we wash ourselves in it, and we scrub our clothes in it. We sail boats in it. We relax and swim in it when it is warm. We skate on it when it is frozen. We use it to make plants grow. Sometimes we drown in it.

Catholics use water in many ways for worship. They pour it on people wanting to become Christian, they sprinkle it at Mass, they dip their fingertips in it to bless themselves, and they drink it with the wine in the chalice.

The frequent use of water in Catholic worship is a token of the waters that Scripture says threaten us in one instant but restore us in the next.

A river flowed out of Eden to water the garden, and from there it divided into four branches (Genesis 2:10). But tempestuous hail and storms of water overwhelm us just as they overwhelmed Israel (Isaiah 28:2, 17; Psalm 69:2, 15).

The Lord always leads us beside still waters, restoring our souls even in death (Psalm 23:2). Jesus gives us water that becomes a spring gushing up to eternal life (John 4:14), and out of the believer's heart flow rivers of living water (John 7:38). In the new Jerusalem, water will spring from the temple near the altar and flow toward the East, nourishing trees and every living creature (Ezekiel 47:1–12). It will be a bright, crystal river, flowing from the throne of God and the Lamb through the middle of the city of God.

The Church uses water generously at baptism, when it is poured on the head of a new believer, or when the baptized is actually immersed in it. The baptismal waters are for a washing and cleansing from sin, and in them the believer dies with Christ.

Since at least the fifth century, Catholics have used water for religious purposes other than baptism. Small fonts containing holy water are commonly located at the entrances to the church. The water in the fonts is called holy because it has been blessed. It has been set apart for religious use by a priest acting in the name of the Church.

A small quantity of salt is sometimes added to holy water. Like the salt once placed on the tongue of the newly baptized as a sign of preservation from evil, salt in the holy water represents our being preserved in the wisdom of Christ.

It is Catholic custom on entering and exiting the church to dip the tips of the fingers of the right hand into the water, and to make the sign of the cross, touching the forehead, the heart, the left shoulder and the right shoulder. The crossing impresses on us the victory won in Christ's death on Calvary. The water recalls our baptismal washing and dying. Holy water has no power in itself. Its use on entering constitutes a ceremonial washing and is an occasion for blessing.

Sometimes at the beginning of Sunday Mass, the priest walks down the aisle of the church sprinkling water on the congregation. The *asperges*, as it is called, or the sprinkling rite, as it is usually called today, replaces the penitential rite. *Asperge* is the first word of the traditional chant sung during the sprinkling: "Purge me, O Lord, with hyssop, and I shall be clean; wash me, and I shall be whiter than snow" (based on Psalm 51:7). During the Easter season the *Vidi aquam* is sung instead. These are the first words of the Latin text, which reads: "I saw water flowing from the right side of the temple. It brought God's life and his salvation, and the people sang in joyful praise: alleluia, alleluia" (based on Ezekiel 47:1–2, 9).

Like the waters of baptism, the asperges signifies our cleansing through God's gracious goodness. The sprinkler used for the purpose is called an *aspergillum*.

The priest adds a little water to the wine in the chalice at Mass. The commingling of water and wine is a token of the commingling of Christ's divinity with his humanity and of our longing to share in Christ's divinity. Tradition says that this water signifies the water that flowed with the blood from the wound in Christ's side (John 19:34). In some depictions of the Crucifixion, the water and the blood from Christ's side are shown spilling into a chalice, from which deer are drinking. The image reflects the opening words of Psalm 42: "As a deer longs for flowing streams, so my soul longs for you, O God."

After the priest has received the people's gifts at Mass, and incensed the gifts and the altar, he washes his hands. The action is symbolic of the priest's desire to be cleansed within.

At funerals the priest sprinkles the coffin with water as a sign of the paschal nature of Christian death and of the promise of eternal life given in baptism. The sprinkling does not symbolize a purification of the deceased.

OIL

An anointing is a ceremonial action performed by the Church to set persons and objects apart from secular use and to obtain for them the benefit of divine grace.

The anointing of priests, prophets, and kings in the Old Testament symbolized their sanctity and their endowment with the Spirit of God. The Israelites referred to their deliverer as the Messiah, the Anointed One.

When Jesus had dinner at the home of Lazarus, his sister Mary anointed Jesus' feet with a costly perfume, filling the house with fragrance (John 12:1–3). The apostles used the title *Christ* to refer to Jesus. Christians therefore understand Christ to be the Messiah, both priest and king.

As early as the seventh century, the anointing of kings and emperors in Europe reflected the influence of the Old Testament anointing of kings. The rite for the coronation of the British monarch includes an anointing even today. Christian baptism has adopted the Old Testament practice of anointing prophets, priests, and kings with oil because they prefigure Christ, the anointed of the Lord.

The ceremony for consecrating the oils takes place at the Chrism Mass which, from 1955, was held in cathedrals on the morning of Holy Thursday, with the clergy of the diocese attending. Today the Chrism Mass may take place at that time, or on another more convenient day. In some dioceses the Chrism Mass has taken on great significance, with many of the laity attending along with the clergy.

The Church uses three oils: the oil of chrism, the oil of catechumens, and the oil of the sick. They are usually reserved in a shallow recess in the sanctuary wall, a small niche like a cupboard. It has a door, often of brass or gold, sometimes engraved with the words *olea sancta*, Latin for "holy oils." In some churches, especially newer ones, the oils are kept in clear glass pitchers or urns and placed in a display case so they are visible.

Usually olive oil is used, but other oils can be used as well. Sometimes bishops in agricultural regions prefer to use oil produced from local crops.

The oil of chrism contains a perfume. It is usually balsam, an oily or gummy resin that comes from various trees and shrubs. The other two oils are not perfumed.

The word *chrism* comes from the Greek word having to do with anointing. The name Christ, originally only a title, means the Anointed One, and is related to the word chrism. The word *Christos* is the Greek translation of the Hebrew word *Messiah*.

The names of the oils suggest their principal uses. The oil of the sick is used to anoint those who seek healing. It can be requested by anyone seeking healing of body, mind, or spirit. The oil is used on occasion for public anointings in church, as well as for individual anointing in hospitals and in the homes of the sick. The New Testament provides examples of anointings of the sick (James 5:14). The oil of the sick is ordinarily blessed by the bishop. In case of necessity it can be blessed by a priest.

The oil of catechumens is used several times during the period of the catechumenate to anoint those preparing for baptism. The priest or deacon anoints the breast, hands, or other parts of the body, as a sign of God's help and strength. The oil strengthens the catechumens' resolve to be free from bonds of the past and to take the step of professing their faith in Christ. The oil of catechumens can be blessed by the bishop or by a priest during the rites of the catechumenate.

The fragrant oil of chrism is the most important of the three oils. It is used for the sacraments of baptism, confirmation, and holy orders. Each of these sacraments confers a seal that marks the recipient forever. As a result these sacraments are conferred only once. The oil of chrism can be consecrated only by a bishop.

At baptism, the chrism is used to anoint the crown of
the head. This anointing is a sign that the baptized is
incorporated into the kingly and prophetic priesthood of
Christ and endowed with the spiritual anointing of the
Holy Spirit.

Chrism is used for confirmation, too, whether it takes
place at the same time as baptism or is delayed till a later
date. Confirmation confers the Holy Spirit upon one who
is a member of Christ. The bishop or priest dips his right
thumb in the chrism and makes the sign of the cross on
the forehead of the confirmand, sealing the believer with
the gift of the Holy Spirit. The oil can also be poured over
the head.

Chrism is also used for the sacrament of holy orders, to
ordain priests in the Church. The bishop spreads chrism
on the hands of the newly ordained priest. Through the
priest's hands the Christian people are sanctified, and sacrifice is offered to God.

Chrism is also used to anoint new altars and churches.
Until recently it was used for the blessing of church bells.

FIRE

Older Catholic churches have an unmistakable smell about
them. It comes from years of burning wax and incense,
mixed perhaps with the smell of old wooden pews and var-
nish. Fire is necessary to make wax, oil, and incense burn.

Fire plays an important role in the worship of the
Church. But at no time does it play a more prominent role
than it does at the Easter Vigil, when the new fire pierces
the deep darkness.

Fire is an important feature in many of the world's
ancient religions. Like the sun, it symbolizes regenerating
warmth and energy. Some religions considered fire an
earthly representative of the sun, and some thought it
actually came from the sun. Illuminated Christmas trees

are a popular remnant of the pagan fire-festivals that took place in the depth of winter to "force" the return of the sun and its warmth.

Besides restoring light and life, fire also can destroy life. It destroyed Sodom and Gomorra in the time of Abraham (Genesis 19:24–29). It destroyed much of London in the seventeenth century, much of the city of Chicago in 1871, and a great part of the city of San Francisco at the time of the great earthquake.

Through its destruction of evil, fire cleanses and purifies. "Wickedness burned like fire" (Isaiah 9:18). The Lord is like a refiner's fire to purify the descendants of Levi, just as it purifies silver and gold (Malachi 3:2–3). Before he responded to God's summons for a spokesman, the prophet Isaiah was first cleansed of his guilt by a burning coal. An angel touched a live coal to his mouth and declared his sin blotted out (Isaiah 6:6–9). Fire represents victory over the forces of darkness.

In the Bible, fire is used as a symbol of God (Deuteronomy 4:24; Psalm 18:12–14; Ezekiel 1:4; Revelation 1:14) and of the Word of God (Jeremiah 23:29). God's anger is a fire (Psalm 18:8), and it burns the land and makes fuel of the evil ones (Isaiah 9:18–19). Before the day of the Lord, the land and its inhabitants will be destroyed in blood, fire, and columns of smoke, except those who call on the name of the Lord (Joel 2:30). At his second coming, Christ will appear in the midst of fire (2 Thessalonians 1:8). Christ and the Holy Spirit are both compared to fire (Malachi 3:2; Matthew 3:11).

The new fire at the Easter Vigil burns in a brazier and presents an astonishing sight in the darkness of the church. The paschal candle is lit from the new fire.

Besides its practical use as a source of light, the flame of a candle or an oil lamp has a mythic and symbolic power as well. It links us with the natural world and its cycles.

With its limited light, a candle hollows out a small, but safe, contained place within the darkness, without completely obliterating it. In fact, its light heightens our awareness of the darkness closing in around us. Seeing the living struggle between the light and the dark, we can know something of the struggle between Christ and the forces of chaos and evil as it plays itself out in the world and within our own hearts and minds.

Light by electricity is now almost universal, and we would find worship at church inconvenient without it. A panel of light switches is quicker and easier, and bulbs are longer-lasting and more dependable than flint, matches, wicks, and oil.

But electric light is static; it does not have the flicker of living flame. And it is powerful enough to reach into the farthest corners. It shines on steps for our safety, and it lights exit doors. It lights up enormous churches to such an extent that the flame of candles is insignificant by comparison.

An overuse of powerful electric lights isolates us from the natural world and reduces the effect of the church's powerful symbolic language. No light bulb can approximate a flame. No flip of a switch can do what the new fire does at the Easter Vigil. Electric vigil lights that light up with the insertion of a coin, and processional candles and altar candles that turn on by the flip of a switch, are no equal to the flame of burning candles.

Light by electricity does not heighten our awareness of darkness. It obliterates it. The Easter Vigil is the only time of the year when we can enter a mythic darkness and see that darkness better by the light of Christ.

INCENSE

The Church also burns incense. Incense is useful in two ways: it gives off smoke, and it produces a sweet fragrance.

Incense is an aromatic gum, spice, or other substance produced by trees or shrubs. The genuine incense is frankincense, a fragrant gum-resin produced by trees native to Somaliland and Southern Arabia. Frankincense was one of the gifts brought by the three Magi to the infant Jesus (Matthew 2:11). But many other types of aromatic substances are burned as well. A non-allergenic variety is now available. Burning incense gives off smoke and a sweet fragrance that fills the church.

The grains of incense are placed on burning charcoal in a metal vessel that sometimes hangs from chains. The top of the vessel is perforated so that the smoke can escape and rise. An acolyte, deacon, or priest swings it during incensation. The vessel itself is known as a *thurible* or a *censer*. The person who carries it is called a *thurifer*.

In the Old Testament, the high priest Aaron was instructed to place two handfuls of incense on the coals in the Temple to produce so much smoke that the cloud of incense would obscure the "mercy-seat," concealing him from the sight of God and protecting his life (Leviticus 16:12–13).

In his vision of the new Jerusalem, Isaiah saw the Lord sitting on a throne in the Temple, attended by angels calling to one another, "Holy, holy, holy is the Lord of hosts; the whole earth is full of his glory." The Temple was filled with smoke (Isaiah 6:1–4).

In one of the visions of Saint John, an angel with a golden censer stands at the altar in the heavenly city, offering a great quantity of incense with the prayers of all the saints (Revelation 8:4). In another, the Temple is filled with smoke from the glory of God and from his power (Revelation 15:8).

The cloud of incense smoke obscures our vision. It drops a veil before our eyes and obscures the splendor of God's glory. We know that in the heavenly city we shall

see the living God face to face, with a beatific vision.
Incense makes our dim vision eager to see the full bril-
liance of God's glory. As the smoke rises, it is reminiscent
of our prayer ascending to God.

Incense was commonly burned as perfume in the
ancient Near East, both in religious and in secular con-
texts. Incense entered the Church's use in imitation of its
use to honor Roman emperors and magistrates. The
Church burns it to signify that Christ's sacrifice and the
Church's worship are a pleasing odor of sweetness
before God.

For centuries the Church used incense at Mass only
during solemn sung celebrations, not at a recited, or less
solemn Mass. Today it can be used at any Eucharist.

Incense is used to incense the altar at the beginning of
Mass, at the procession and proclamation of the Gospel, at
the preparation of the gifts (to incense the gifts, the altar,
the priest, and people), and at the elevation of the
eucharistic bread and chalice after the consecration.

At funerals, the priest uses incense during the final
commendation and farewell as a sign of respect for the
deceased's body as a temple of the Holy Spirit.

Incense is commonly used at evening prayer during the
singing of Psalm 141: "Let my prayer be counted as
incense before you, and the lifting up of my hands as an
evening sacrifice."

Perhaps the largest thurible ever used is the one at the
cathedral of Santiago de Compostela in Spain, the leg-
endary burial place of the apostle James. During the Middle Ages, his shrine was the destination of pilgrims from
all over Europe. On his feast day, July 25, the *botafumeiro*,
an enormous censer, is suspended by rope from the ceiling
of the nave. Standing nearly five feet high, it takes a number of men pulling on the rope to make it swing from one
transept to another.

Besides burning wax and incense, the Church also burns the palms remaining from the previous year's Palm Sunday. The ashes are used on Ash Wednesday to mark the foreheads of Catholics with a sign of the cross, a reminder that we are dust and will return to dust.

9 Vestments

The vestments that the clergy and ministers wear contribute to the festive character of Catholic worship. Their exotic shapes and designs distinguish them from ordinary street dress, although at their origin they were just the best of ordinary street clothes. Some of them have complex and interesting histories. Their colors change according to the season or feast. They are much more than just visual aids or imaginative costumes. They contribute to the beauty of worship.

Some vestments have a technical significance that identifies the wearer's place in the Church's hierarchy. The diversity of ministries in the Church is shown outwardly in the diversity of vestments.

The colors traditionally used in Roman Catholic worship are white, red, violet, black, green, and rose.

White is used for the Easter and Christmas seasons, on feasts of the Lord (other than his passion), on feasts of Mary, the angels, saints who were not martyrs, All Saints Day (November 1), and on the feasts of Saint John the Baptist, Saint John the Evangelist, the Chair of Saint Peter, and the Conversion of Saint Paul. White is now also common for funerals. Gold vestments are sometimes used on solemnities instead of white.

Red vestments are used on Palm Sunday, Good Friday, Pentecost, celebrations of the Lord's passion, birthday feasts of the apostles and evangelists, and feasts of martyrs.

Violet is used in Lent and Advent. It can also be worn for funerals. Black may also be used for funerals.

Rose vestments may replace violet vestments on the third Sunday of Advent (called *Gaudete* Sunday for the first word of the Gregorian entrance chant: "Rejoice in the Lord always; again I say, rejoice") and on the fourth Sunday of Lent (called *Laetare* Sunday for the first word of the Gregorian entrance chant: "Rejoice, Jerusalem . . . rejoice with gladness").

Green is used during Ordinary Time, that is, during the season after Epiphany and the season after Pentecost.

The stole, the chasuble, and dalmatic change color with the season or feast. The alb is always white.

THE ALB

The most basic of all the vestments is the alb. It reaches from the neck to the ankles. It has long, close-fitting sleeves and is tied at the waist with a rope-like cincture. The alb is worn by liturgical ministers of every rank, both ordained and lay, including the bishop, the priest, the deacon, acolytes, crucifers (cross bearers), and thurifers. Some cantors and choirs also wear the alb. The name of the vestment comes from the Latin word for its color, *alba*, or "white."

The alb is derived from the tunic common in the ancient Roman world and has been used in Christian worship from very early times.

When the women went to the tomb on Easter Day, they were met by an angel dressed in white, who told them that Jesus had risen from death (Matthew 28:3). In the heavenly city, a great multitude of the redeemed from every nation, from all tribes and peoples and languages, stand before the throne and before the Lamb, robed in white, and they cry out, saying, "Salvation belongs to our God" (Revelation 7:9–10).

THE STOLE

The stole is a long narrow strip of fabric worn around the neck. It is the vestment proper to ordained bishops, priests, and deacons and is a symbol of the sacramental and teaching authority of people in holy orders. It is never worn by laity. The stole takes the color of the season or feast.

The deacon wears the stole like a sash over his left shoulder, draws it across the chest to the right side, and fastens it below the right arm. The bishop and the priest wear the stole around their neck, with its ends falling down in front. The priest wears the stole for administering all the sacraments, and often for preaching.

THE CHASUBLE

The chasuble is the ample outer garment worn by bishops and priests celebrating the Eucharist and while presiding at other rites immediately connected with it. Its beauty and dignity contribute to the solemnity of eucharistic worship. In its so-called Roman shape, it is rather like a tent, with a hole for the head. It looks like a poncho and is derived from the outdoor cloak of both men and women in the later Graeco-Roman world. The chasuble represents the charity of Christ that covers all things (Colossians 3:14).

The modern artist Henri Matisse designed a resplendent set of chasubles for a Dominican convent in France. They have been called the handsomest ecclesiastical raiment made in France since the sixteenth century.

The chasuble common until Vatican II was the fiddleback design, so called for its similarity to the shape of a violin. It hung over the shoulders, down the front and the back, but with the sides cut away, exposing the arms.

THE DALMATIC

The outer garment proper to deacons is called the dalmatic. It is a tunic derived from a garment popular among the upper classes in Rome in the second century. Its characteristic feature is the two stripes of colored material that run vertically on the front and back, from top to bottom and over the shoulders. The dalmatic is optional and is often used only on more solemn occasions. Both the dalmatic and the chasuble take the color of the season or feast.

THE SURPLICE

The surplice is an adaptation of the alb and has wider, looser-fitting sleeves. In earlier centuries, the surplice accommodated itself over the fur coats customary in cold churches of the northern countries in earlier centuries. Albs were less suitable. This explains the garment's name, which comes from the Latin *superpelliceum*, "over the fur." The surplice is always white.

From the Middle Ages, the surplice was the dress of the clergy in lower ranks, and it came to be used also by priests outside of Mass. Originally reaching to the ankles, like the alb, it grew shorter over time. In some places it reached just below the waist. Its sleeves were also shortened. Choir boys and choir girls sometimes wear these shortened surplices.

The surplice is sometimes still worn by choirs, in token of the fact that for centuries choirs were staffed by clerics and by boys being groomed for service in the Church.

The priest wears the stole over the surplice for the administration of the sacraments outside Mass, especially for the sacrament of reconciliation. The surplice is not worn for Mass.

THE PALL

The pall is the large flat cloth that covers the coffin at funerals. Its color is commonly white, purple, or black.

We are not accustomed to think of the pall as a vestment. But the pall is a symbol of the white garment of salvation in which the deceased was cloaked at baptism.

10 The Crucifix

The crucifix is the sculpted image of Christ on the cross. It may show the suffering Christ, the dead Christ with a wound in his side, or Christ the king in priestly vestments. Along with the Christ resurrected in glory, the crucifix is the central image of Christian belief. Through baptism Christians die with Christ and rise with him in the Resurrection.

There is a technical difference between a crucifix and a cross. The difference has been reflected in the differing piety of Catholics and non-Catholics.

The crucifix includes the *corpus*, the body of Christ. It is found in some Lutheran and Episcopal churches, but it has played a particularly important role in Catholic piety. Many Protestant Churches have preferred the cross, without a corpus, because the empty cross more adequately expresses Christ's victory over death.

Catholic devotional life has shifted emphasis in recent decades. For centuries, Catholic piety focused so exclusively on the passion and death of Christ that his resurrection and ascension were diminished.

Catholic piety today has an increasingly paschal character. It appreciates that Christ had to endure the sufferings of the cross before he could be glorified.

11 The Tabernacle

The tabernacle is an ornamented, solid, and opaque receptacle where the vessels containing the Blessed Sacrament are reserved. Some tabernacles are covered with a veil. A lamp or candle burns continuously before the tabernacle as a sign of the presence of the Lord. To express their reverence for this most holy Sacrament, Catholics traditionally genuflect when passing in front of the tabernacle.

The word tabernacle comes from the Latin word for a tent. In the Old Testament the tabernacle was the portable shrine that went with the Israelites on their wilderness wanderings. It housed the ark, the seven-branched lamp stand, the table for the 12 loaves, the altar of incense, and the altar of sacrifice (Exodus 25–31 and 35–40). The tabernacle embodied the presence of God in the midst of the Israelites.

The tabernacle in Catholic churches has a clear similarity to the Hebrew tabernacle. Both symbolize the presence of God.

From the sixteenth century, in some places, the tabernacle came to be set in the middle of the high altar. Today the tabernacle is usually kept on a side altar, or in a separate chapel, sometimes on a pedestal instead of an altar. In keeping with the nature of the eucharistic meal, the sacramental bread is not usually kept on the altar where Mass is celebrated.

In Saint Peter's Basilica the tabernacle was designed by Bernini, the great Renaissance sculptor-architect, in the likeness of a temple. It is not located on the high altar but in a side chapel.

Catholics are among few Christian bodies that reserve the eucharistic bread and wine after Mass is over. The practice enables the Sacrament to be taken to the sick and the homebound who are unable to participate in the Eucharist with the rest of the congregation.

Devotion to the Sacrament has no equal in the personal and public piety of Roman Catholics. On occasions like the Solemnity of the Body and Blood of Christ, formerly known by its Latin name, *Corpus Christi*, the sacrament is often removed from the tabernacle and exposed for public adoration. For this purpose, a host of sacramental bread is placed in a decorated vessel called a monstrance, where the Sacrament can be seen more easily.

The town of Bethlehem, the birthplace of Jesus, takes its name from two Hebrew words meaning "house of bread." The tabernacle that holds the body of the Lord in a Catholic church is a type of Bethlehem, a house of bread.

12 The Stations of the Cross

The stations of the cross are the series of usually 14 paintings, sculptures, or carvings placed around a church's walls. They depict particular moments in Christ's journey from Pilate's house to his burial.

The stations are a popular private devotion, but communal stations of the cross often take place during Lent. The devotion involves walking from one station to the next, reciting prayers and meditating on each event.

The practice probably arose out of the early custom of pilgrims to Jerusalem walking the traditional route from Pilate's house to Calvary. The Franciscans popularized the devotion in the later Middle Ages.

The modern American painter Barnett Newman produced a remarkable series of stark, abstract works for the stations of the cross. Each station features a single, sharp vertical stripe dividing a solid field. No human figures are pictured, nor even a cross. The stripes have been compared to God's primal act of creation and to the separation of light from dark.

13 Statues, Pictures, Icons, and Stained Glass

In the Apostles' Creed, Christians declare their belief in the communion of saints, the spiritual union existing among all Christians, both the living and the dead, and between them and Christ. It is a source of comfort and hope for the living. The statues and other images of the saints in Catholic churches are signs of the communion of saints. The persons represented in wood and stone, glass and paint, hold a place of honor in the Church. Because of their closeness to God and their accessibility to our humanity, they play a role in the communion of saints. They make intercession with us through Christ, to the Father of mercies. The practice of venerating and invoking the saints has been a part of Catholic devotion from the earliest times.

The veneration that Catholics show to the saints does not replace the all-important worship that they offer to God the Father through Christ in the Holy Spirit, nor does it compete with it. The veneration of the saints has its foundation in Saint Paul's doctrine of the Mystical Body of Christ (Romans 12:4–8), in which all members have their particular office to fulfill as "citizens with the saints and also members of the household of God" (Ephesians 2:19).

Christ himself promises special privileges to certain persons in the next world (Matthew 19:28). And the story of Dives and Lazarus suggests that the dead may intercede on behalf of the living (Luke 16:19–31).

The early Christians observed the anniversary of the death date of the martyrs. The practice developed into the veneration of the relics of all who had died for their faith. Catholics believe that the prayer of the saints is efficacious as long as they follow in their footsteps.

Statues, pictures, icons, and images in glass give us a place in the communion of saints.

14 Symbols of Christ, the Holy Spirit, and the Trinity

A variety of symbols and monograms are sewn onto vestments, banners and veils, carved into wood and stone, painted into glass, or fashioned out of precious metal.

The monogram of a large P superimposed over a large X represents Christ. Called the Chi-Rho, the X and P are the first two letters of the Greek name for Christ: *XPISTOS*.

The letters INRI often appear on the top of crucifixes. They are the first letters of the Latin inscription that was placed on the cross of Jesus: *Iesus Nazarenus Rex Judaeorum*. It translates: Jesus of Nazareth, King of the Jews (John 19:19–21).

The monogram IHS represents the first three capital letters of the Greek name for Jesus: *IHSOUS*.

The first and last letters of the Greek alphabet, A and Ω, symbolize Christ, the alpha and the omega, the first and the last, the beginning and the end (Revelation 1:8; 21:6; 22:13), who is all and in all (Colossians 3:11).

The image of the fish appears in the catacombs and in other early Christian art and literature. It is a common symbol for Christ, for Christians, and for the Eucharist. Christ shared meals of fish with his followers, as well as meals of bread.

The Greek word for fish is *ichthus*. Christians use it as an acronym. Each letter represents the first letter of the Greek words for: Jesus Christ, Son of God, Savior.

The image of the fish, therefore, signifies the communion of Christians in Christ. From early times Christians ate fish instead of meat on days of abstinence.

The pelican is another image of Christ. Legend holds that the mother pelican pierces her breast with her beak in order to feed her young. Like the pelican, Christ gives his blood for the spiritual nourishment of his followers.

The dove is a common image of the Holy Spirit. The Holy Spirit descended in the likeness of a dove when Jesus was baptized in the Jordan.

In biblical usage, the eye is not only the organ of vision, but it serves as a figure for the entire person. Likewise, the eye of God represents the entire person of God the Father. More than our own eyes, the eyes of God observe all things (Proverbs 15:3). An eye is often shown with a dove above depictions of the Crucifixion. Together they signify the Trinity.

The triangle is another common symbol for the Trinity: Father, Son, and Holy Spirit.

Conclusion

The paschal mystery of Christ deals with the mysteries of life and death as Christ experienced them and interpreted them for his followers. It is not easily explained or quickly defined. In fact, the paschal mystery is more easily lived and experienced through symbols and images than it is defined or described in words. Through its vocabulary of signs and symbols, Catholicism makes the living Christ tangible and accessible to people everywhere.

No matter how young or old you are, no matter what your past or future may be, you can enter the rich symbolism of Catholic worship and, by participating fully, consciously, and actively in the sacred mysteries, know firsthand the power and glory of Christ's paschal mystery.